Snow White Special

A Dwarf Panto of a Minidrama

Richard Tydeman

A SAMUEL FRENCH ACTING EDITION

SAMUEL FRENCH

FOUNDED 1830

SAMUELFRENCH-LONDON.CO.UK
SAMUELFRENCH.COM

CHARACTERS

(in the order of their appearance)

THE COMPERE, *who has a book*
GUSTAV, *the Royal Wizard's Assistant*
JAYBEE, *the Royal Wizard himself*
SNOW WHITE, *a Very Special Laundry-Maid*
QUEEN ERMYNTRUDE, *a Wicked Aunt*
TWO ATTENDANTS, *male or female*
THE SEVEN DWARFS,
    Monday, Tuesday, Wednesday, Thursday,
    Friday, Saturday and Sunday

SCENES: The Magic Mirror Room at the Palace, and the Dwarfs' Cottage.

SNOW WHITE SPECIAL

The COMPERE, *carrying a copy of the script, appears before the curtain.*

COMPERE.   Kind friends, I pray you, give me time
To introduce our Pantomime.
It's very short—and what is worse—
It's written in atrocious verse.
(I hope the acting's not the same,
Or else you'll wish you never came!)
You've read, of course, in story books,
About the girl whose beauteous looks
And Persil-washed complexion bright
Have earned for her the name "Snow White."
Those story books you must not heed,
They are not truthful; no indeed,
Such tales no thinking person swallows!
The *real* story is as follows:—
Act One. A palace. Long ago.
The curtain rises now, to show
    (*Curtain rises.* GUSTAV *is busy with something that looks
like a primitive wireless set with many loose wires, behind a
large gauze-covered picture frame—the "magic mirror."*)
    Gustav, the Royal Wizard's mate.

GUSTAV.   Cor flip, I 'ope the boss ain't late;
I don't know 'ow to work the doin's.
    (*There is a flash or bang from* GUSTAV'S *apparatus.*)

COMPERE.   This lad will have the place in ruins!
What is this strange contraption, sirrah?

GUSTAV.   It's s'posed to be a magic mirror.

COMPERE.   Ah yes. Good friends, you've heard about
This magic glass, I have no doubt.
The Queen consults it every day,
And presently you'll hear her say:—
"Mirror, mirror, on the wall,
Who is the fairest one of all?"
To which replies the looking-glass:—
"Your Majesty doth all surpass."
This interesting little custom
We'll now observe.
    (*A bigger flash or bang from the apparatus.*)

GUSTAV.   Oh 'eck, I've bust 'em!

COMPERE.   What *are* you doing?

GUSTAV.   I dunno,
I just can't get the thing to go.

COMPERE.	But here comes real cause for worry—
	Jaybee the Wizard, in a hurry.
	(Enter JAYBEE, the Royal Wizard.)
JAYBEE.	Come, switch on quick, and help me in it.
	We'll have the Queen here any minute.
	(He starts to get behind the "mirror.")
COMPERE.	Good sir, your bold assistant here
	Has got into a mess, I fear.
JAYBEE.	Oh no! I told him how to work it.
GUSTAV.	Five valves gone west on one short circuit.
JAYBEE.	You surely can't have broken five!
	(He reaches into the apparatus.)
GUSTAV.	Look out, I think that wire's alive.
	(JAYBEE jumps back and hops about sucking fingers.)
JAYBEE.	Of all the stupid blundering dolts,
	You've filled my fingers full of volts!
	(Exit JAYBEE, R.)
COMPERE.	While Jaybee goes to seek first-aid,
	In comes Snow White, the laundry maid.
	(Enter SNOW WHITE, R.)
	Our Gustav rises to his feet;
	He feels his heart begin to beat.
	(And we can hear his heart beating; drum in the wings.)
SNOW WHITE.	Whatever's bitten poor Jaybee?
GUSTAV.	He isn't very pleased with me.
COMPERE.	And that is quite—I sadly fear—
	The understatement of the year.
	The maid advances to the table
	Where Gustav shows the offending cable.
	Her nimble fingers deftly fix
	The wires inside the box of tricks;
	And now she straightens up to say:—
SNOW WHITE.	I think you'll find that's quite O.K.
COMPERE.	As Gustav gazes at her proudly.
	His heart is beating very loudly.
	(And so is the drum in the wings.)
	And bowing in a manner dashing,
	He says:—
GUSTAV.	Cor flip, I think you're smashing!
COMPERE.	A compliment, I would have said,
	That might be misinterpreted.
	But Gustav's heart has ceased to beat,
	For he has heard the sound of feet
	Approaching with a regal tread.
GUSTAV.	The Queen!
SNOW WHITE.	All right, don't lose your head.
COMPERE.	So saying, this resourceful dame
	Shoves Gustav in the picture-frame,

And giving him a loving look
She starts to check the laundry-book.
(SNOW WHITE *is checking laundry down* L. GUSTAV, C., *is
behind the "magic mirror". Enter,* R., *two* ATTENDANTS *walking
backwards in front of the* QUEEN.)

1ST ATTEND.   Make way, make way, and bow the knee
   Before Her Gracious Majesty,
2ND ATTEND.   Queen Ermyntrude, the Queen of Beauty.
QUEEN.   I thank you both; you've done your duty.
1ST ATTEND.   Be silent all before the Queen.
QUEEN.   All right.
2ND ATTEND.   And let no frowns be seen.
1ST ATTEND.   Her Majesty with joy shall fill you.
QUEEN.   All right.
2ND ATTEND.   Make way—
QUEEN.   Oh shut up, will you!
COMPERE.   The questioning's about to start.
   (Let's hope that Gustav's learnt his part!)
   With carriage proud, and step serene,
   Towards the mirror moves the Queen.
QUEEN.   Mirror, mirror on the wall,
   Who is the fairest one of all?
COMPERE.   Instead of Jaybee's prompt reply,
   The mirror seems to give a sigh
   As Gustav bites his bottom lip
   And softly murmers:—
GUSTAV.   Ooh, cor flip.
COMPERE.   Impatiently the Queen once more
   Repeats the question as before.
QUEEN.   Mirror, mirror on the wall,
   Who is the fairest one of all?
SNOW WHITE   *(prompting in a whisper).*
   Your Majesty doth all surpass.
GUSTAV.   Your Majesty's as bold as brass.
SNOW WHITE   *(still whispering).*
   No, no, I never told you that!
GUSTAV.   I mean you're very old and fat.
QUEEN   *(angrily).* What's this?
SNOW WHITE   *(in an anxious whisper).* Do get the answer right!
GUSTAV.   I mean the fairest one's Snow White.
QUEEN.   So ho! My magic mirror rare,
   You think my laundry-maid is fair?
   This day for her shall be the last.
   Seize yonder maid and hold her fast.
   (*The* ATTENDANTS *seize* SNOW WHITE.)
   In darkest forest set her free,
   About the time the lions have tea.
   I think we'll find that by tonight

                    Only her bones will still be white!
          (*Exit* QUEEN R. *with a horrible laugh.*)
COMPERE.   Exit the Queen, with horrid laughter.
                   Snow White is quickly hustled after.
          (ATTENDANTS *take* SNOW WHITE *off* R.)
                   As Gustav cries in sore distress: —
GUSTAV.   Cor Lumme, what a flipping mess!
          (*The curtain falls, leaving the* COMPERE *outside.*)
COMPERE.   Far off they take the hapless maid,
                   And dump her in a forest glade
                   Where hungry creatures have their lairs,
                   And leave her to the lions and bears.
                   But near that spot, among the trees
                   A funny little house she sees,
                   With seven chimneys in a row,
                   And seven little windows low,
                   And seven little rooms inside;
                   For there the Seven Dwarfs reside.
                   And here they are, their day's work done,
                   Arriving home at set of sun.
                   (They're really little tiny men,
                   The tallest only two foot ten;
                   But so as not to hurt your eyes,
                   We've magnified them double size.)

(The curtain rises to show interior of Dwarfs' Cottage. A table; a bench or boxes to sit on; an imitation T.V. set down L. *March. Enter the* SEVEN DWARFS—*but see Production Notes for instructions if less than seven available.*)

                   Good evening to you, little elves;
                   Perhaps you'll introduce yourselves
MONDAY.   Seven little Dwarfs are we.
TUESDAY.   Nicer Dwarfs you'll never sec.
WEDNESDAY.   Our names are: —Wednesday,
TUESDAY.   Tuesday,
MONDAY.   Monday,
THURSDAY.   Thursday,
FRIDAY.   Friday,
SATURDAY.   Saturday,
SUNDAY.   Sunday.
COMPERE.   Delightful names; they suit you well;
                   But how you got them, who can tell?
WEDNESDAY.   The reason's not so hard to seek:
                   You see, we're just a little weak.
THURSDAY.   The Magistrate—to coin a phrase—
                   Told Dad he'd give him seven days.
FRIDAY.   Dad says our names remind him still
                   Of holidays in Pentonville.
SATURDAY.   So now our story we've repeated.

COMPERE.   I thank you, Dwarfs. Do please be seated.

(Opportunity here for funny business. E.g.—They all sit, but MONDAY *sits on the second seat instead of the first, and therefore* SUNDAY *has no seat and falls on floor. He gets up and pushes* SATURDAY, *who pushes* FRIDAY, *etc. Eventually* MONDAY *moves on to first seat and all move up one. Meantime,* SUNDAY *moves round to other end of line, just as they have all moved along. He pushes* MONDAY, *etc., and all move down again. Meanwhile,* SUNDAY *goes back to the other end just as they have all moved along. He scratches his head, gives* SATURDAY *a big push; all move along, and* SUNDAY *sits.)*

Ah good. That's better. Now let's hear
How things are going.

MONDAY.   Bad, I fear.
TUESDAY.   Our tyres are flat; our bikes have rusted;
WEDNESDAY.   The lights have fused; the T.V's busted;
THURSDAY.   The copper kettle's sprung a leak;
FRIDAY.   The mangle's got an awful squeak;
SATURDAY.   The paper off the walls is peeling,
SUNDAY.   There's death watch beetle in the ceiling.
MONDAY.   The ugly truth we'll have to face:
We need a man about the place.
(All shake their heads sadly.)

TUESDAY.   Well, now we've said our little piece,
It's time to go and feed the geese.
THURSDAY.   And wrap some leather round our legs.
FRIDAY.   And search the nettle patch for eggs.
SATURDAY.   Each take a stick, and if attacked
You all know how you ought to act.
(They rise and arm themselves with sticks.)
COMPERE.   So now the Dwarfs their weapons take.
It seems a lot of fuss to make;
It really looks a bit absurd
To go out armed against a bird.
SUNDAY.   Now look here mate, before you chide us,
Don't forget you've magnified us.
If you could come outside, you'd see
The gander's twice as big as me.
COMPERE.   Of course, I'd quite forgotten that.
Well, do be careful what you're at.
(Exit DWARFS, R.*)*
So off they go with courage rash,
To give the geese their daily mash.
But hardly have they left before
A knock sounds at the other door,
And seeking shelter for the night
Appears our heroine, Snow White.
(Enter SNOW WHITE, L.*)*

> She scarcely can believe her eyes,
> And looks around in great surprise.

SNOW WHITE. This place is in a shocking state.
I'll have to try and put it straight.

(During the next speech, SNOW WHITE moves quickly about the stage cleaning and repairing imaginary articles.)

COMPERE. Then, in a most efficient manner
She fetches out her pocket spanner,
Pliers, screw-driver, oilcan,
To make the place look spick and span.
In less time than it takes to tell,
The T.V. set is working well;
The mangle's had a lovely oiling;
The mended copper kettle's boiling;
The house is clean from floor to thatch;
The death watch beetle's met his match;
While seven bikes, with tyres inflated,
Stand gleaming as if silver-plated.
(I trust that your imagination
Can cope with such a situation?)

(Exit SNOW WHITE L.)

Exhausted now, the maiden goes
Upstairs to seek well-earned repose
And rest her weary feet and legs.
Re-enter Dwarfs, with goose's eggs.

(Re-enter DWARFS R. carrying enormous eggs. They gaze about.)

> They gaze around in consternation
> At such a wondrous transformation,
> And blink at all the shining metal
> On mangle, bikes and copper kettle.

MONDAY. Whoever could have been in here?
TUESDAY. There's more than one; that's very clear.
WEDNESDAY. Perhaps they sent the army?
THURSDAY. Yes,
Or else the W.V.S.
FRIDAY. No mortals work at such a pace;
They must have come from Outer Space.
SATURDAY. The house has never looked so clean;
SUNDAY. And "Six-Five Special's" on the screen!

(All crowd round T.V. set as SUNDAY turns volume up and music is heard. Opportunity for dance, skiffle group, etc.)

COMPERE. Awakened by the noisy din,
Snow White now quickly hurries in.

(Enter SNOW WHITE L. They switch off T.V. and stare.)

SNOW WHITE. Now then, you naughty little boys,
Stop making all that dreadful noise.
COMPERE. At first this makes the Dwarfs defiant:

TUESDAY.	We're not afraid of you, you giant!
	(But they all try to hide behind each other.)
COMPERE.	Then, noticing her box of tools,
	The leader cries:
MONDAY.	What silly fools
	We are to get in such a panic;
	This must be our unknown mechanic!
COMPERE.	Snow White admits that this is true.
SNOW WHITE.	I'd like to stay and work for you.
COMPERE.	The Dwarfs all try to make amends,
	And soon they are the best of friends,
	They turn the music on once more,
	And all together take the floor.

(SUNDAY turns music on again and all dance, etc. Curtain slowly falls, leaving COMPERE outside. Music dies away.)

So thus Snow White the office took
Of foster-mother, housewife, cook,
Of electrician, engineer—
And time ran on for half a year.
Meanwhile within the palace grey,
Poor Gustav nearly pined away.
But now the Queen begins to hear
Reports that fill her heart with fear:
Within the forest, so 'tis said,
There dwells a maid who's far from dead,
And every day her beauty grows.
The jealous Queen with anger glows;
Proceeding to disguise herself,
She takes an apple from the shelf,
Scoops out the fruit and puts inside
Potassium of cyanide!
So, as the curtain once more rises,
Prepare yourselves for more surprises.

(Curtain rises. SNOW WHITE is sitting in a chair, C., reading to the DWARFS who are sitting on the floor.)

SNOW WHITE.	So Sleeping Beauty came to life
	And soon became the Prince's wife.
	The palace rang with joy and laughter,
	And all lived happy ever after.

(She closes the book.)

TUESDAY.	Oh, don't stop yet! We'll all be good.
WEDNESDAY.	Please read about Red Riding Hood.
THURSDAY.	Or Goldilocks who met the bears.
SNOW WHITE.	No no, it's time to go upstairs.

(DWARFS all sigh, rise, and say goodnight.)

Good night then, Wednesday, Tuesday, Monday,
Thursday, Friday, Saturday, Sunday.

(DWARFS *exit up* L.)

COMPERE. So off they go. And Snow White, yawning,
Goes off as well, to sleep till morning.

(SNOW WHITE *yawns and exits up* L. *Enter* R. *the* QUEEN,
in cloak and hood, carrying an apple.)

But who is this, so darkly gliding,
Beneath her cloak an apple hiding?
Yes, yes, I'm sure you've recognised
The bad Queen Ermyntrude, disguised.

QUEEN. I say Snow White shall die! So be it.
I'll leave this apple where she'll see it.
One bite of this, however small,
And *I'll* be fairest one of all.

(*She leaves apple on chair and exits with low chuckle.*)

COMPERE. But little has the Queen divined
That someone else is close behind,
And hardly has she left the place,
When round the corner comes the face
Of faithful Gustav, all suspicious,
(*Enter* GUSTAV, R., *cautiously.*)
He sees the apple so delicious;
He lifts the poison to his nose,
Inhales the fumes, and down he goes!

(GUSTAV *smells apple, and making a lot of noise, falls
unconscious in the chair, with apple still held to nose.*)

The noise he makes is so distressing
That down the stairs the Dwarfs come pressing.

(*Re-enter* DWARFS. GUSTAV *is now stiff and silent.*)

They gaze in horror at the sight,
And one runs off to fetch Snow White.
(*Exit* SUNDAY.)

MONDAY. Another giant! Dead, I fear.
I wish he hadn't died in here.
TUESDAY. He's such a size! We'll never lift him.
WEDNESDAY. We'll have to cut him up to shift him.
THURSDAY. I'll get a knife. (*Exit.*)
FRIDAY. I'll get a spade.
SATURDAY. I'll go and get a coffin made.
TUESDAY. I wonder if he's Church or Chapel?
(*Re-enter* SNOW WHITE *and* SUNDAY.)

COMPERE. But Snow White enters, takes the apple,
Throws it away, and with a sigh
Our Gustav opens half an eye.
Then opens both.
THURSDAY (*re-entering*). Now here's a knife.
WEDNESDAY. Too late; I think he's come to life.
SNOW WHITE. Tell them you've come to life, dear Gustav.
GUSTAV. Cor flip, well yes, I s'pose I must have.

COMPERE. With that, he takes his lady's hand.
The tactful Dwarfs all understand.
    (*The* DWARFS *turn away with their hands clasped behind them, whistling.*)
When through the window, suddenly
Appears the Wizard, old Jaybee.
    (*Enter* JAYBEE, *preferably through the audience.*)
He carries in his hand two scrolls
Which now he carefully unrolls.

JAYBEE. This parchment proves,

COMPERE.   He says,

JAYBEE.   that you,
Gustav, are King of Timbuctoo!
While Snow White here is nothing less
Than Lady Blanche, the Crown Princess.
    (*Re-enter* QUEEN. *She kneels and offers* SNOW WHITE *a bright yellow cardboard crown.*)

QUEEN. My child, forgive your wicked aunt.
I tried to kill you, but I can't.
So take my crown—I've had it sprayed,
And I will be your laundry-maid.
    (*Tableau. The two* ATTENDANTS *enter with a crown for* GUSTAV, *or orb and sceptre, etc.*)

COMPERE. Well, all this is, as you can see,
Extremely satisfactory.
Snow White and Gustav now can wed,
And occupy the throne instead.
So that's the *real* tale, my friends,
And there, I fear, our story ends.

MONDAY. I say, I hate to make a fuss,
But haven't you forgotten us?

COMPERE. Ah yes, the Dwarfs; I beg your pardon.
In every small suburban garden
Your figures shall for ever be
Found standing round the rockery.
So finishes my humble task;
To give the final word I'll ask.
King Gustav and Her Ladyship.

SNOW WHITE. I'll say Good night.

GUSTAV.   I'll say—(*He is tongue-tied*)—Cor flip!

CURTAIN.

(Production notes at end of play.)

9

PRODUCTION NOTES

Those who have already produced other Minidramas will hardly need Production Notes for this one. Briefly, everything has been kept to a minimum, of words to learn, scenery and props., costume-making, and stage directions. The enterprising producer is left a very free hand! Play at a good pace, with everyone saying the exact words allotted to them, neither more nor less, to bring out the full "atrocity" of the verse.

The Magic Mirror merely needs a large picture frame covered with gauze, set at an angle so that the audience can see GUSTAV behind it, but the QUEEN cannot. The T.V. set in the Dwarfs' Cottage can be a large cardboard box, so that the "screen" is turned away from the audience.

Costumes can be "fairy story" type, concocted from the wardrobe and the rag-bag. The DWARFS can be as big as you like, and the bigger they are the funnier it will be. Dress them as much alike as possible, preferably like those little terra-cotta rockery ornaments, with pointed red hats and Wellington boots.

If your company cannot manage as many as Seven Dwarfs, you can play the piece with only Four—Monday, Wednesday, Friday and Sunday, sharing the others' lines among them. In this case, put large labels on them, saying "1," "3," "5" and "7," and insert the following lines after "Seven Little Dwarfs are we: Nicer Dwarfs you'll never see.":—

COMPERE. Did you say Seven? Are you sure?
          To me it only looks like four.

MONDAY.   We had to come without our mates;
          No Parking here on Even Dates.

This Minidrama is designed for a mixed cast, but it can just as easily be played by all men or all women if preferred.—R.T.

www.ingramcontent.com/pod-product-compliance
Ingram Content Group UK Ltd.
Pitfield, Milton Keynes, MK11 3LW, UK
UKHW021818150726
7214IPUK00017B/189